T0107440

WestBow Press books may be ordered through booksellers or by contacting:

WestBow Press
A Division of Thomas Nelson & Zondervan
1663 Liberty Drive
Bloomington, IN 47403
www.westbowpress.com
1 (866) 928-1240

Because of the dynamic nature of the Internet, any web addresses or
links contained in this book may have changed since publication and
may no longer be valid. The views expressed in this work are solely those
of the author and do not necessarily reflect the views of the publisher,
and the publisher hereby disclaims any responsibility for them.

Any people depicted in stock imagery provided by Thinkstock are models,
and such images are being used for illustrative purposes only.
Certain stock imagery © Thinkstock.

ISBN: 978-1-4908-3685-0 (sc)
ISBN: 978-1-4908-3684-3 (e)

Library of Congress Control Number: 2014940108

Printed in the United States of America.

WestBow Press rev. date: 07/23/2014

Life's Little Frustrations

A *Just-for-Fun Book*

Mary Love Eyster

WESTBOW°
P R E S S
A DIVISION OF THOMAS NELSON
& ZONDERVAN

A Word from the Author

Sometimes it is easier for me to express my feelings in poetry form than in prose. As I was thinking one day about some of life's aggravations and irritations, I began jotting down the verses contained in this book. They express my own frustrations over some small incidents that have been labeled "bumps in the road." We are all a part of the human condition and regularly encounter circumstances that hinder our progress and try our patience. I share these thoughts believing that readers will relate because we all encounter some of the same or similar experiences. Hopefully, we will gain perspective as we chuckle over these minor annoyances of life remembering that "a merry heart doeth good like a medicine." (Proverbs 17:22, KVJ)

Special thanks go to Melissa Dees for her technological assistance, editing, and encouragement, and to my daughter, Weety Vickery, for drawing the picture for the front cover.

--Mary Love Eyster

Life's Little
Frustrations

I wonder how the chewing gum
That other people chew
Always seems to end up
On the bottom of *my* shoe.

Out of the corner of my eye,
I see a fly go buzzing by.
I swat him dead; then chortle I,
"The hand is quicker than the fly!"

I wanted to buy something
the other day,
But the cashier said,
"There's just no way."
Then she explained,
with a worried frown,
"We can't sell.
The computer's down!"

You have a doctor's appointment,
And you're afraid you will be late,
So you rush around and hurry up
Just so you can wait.

I'm slow to adopt new fashion trends.
About the time I do, that fad ends,
But I wear it with a great big smile,
Unaware that it's gone out of style!

Today I went out
shopping for shoes,
And I really didn't know
which to choose—
The heels that were
so pretty and pert
Or the simple flats
that didn't hurt!

I reached in my purse
and pulled out a pen.
I pressed it to the paper,
moved it, but then
No mark was there,
a discouraging sight.
I just hate a pen
that will not write!

I drove into the drive-through
and placed an order there.
I rode up to the window,
then entirely unaware,
Until I opened the sack of food
for which I had just paid,
That I received the order that
another person made!

There was a sliver of soap left over
after my bath today.
It's not enough to use again,
but I hate to throw it away.
I'd put it with some other slivers,
but I do not have a stash.
Should I start saving slivers or
just throw it in the trash?

I came home hot and thirsty too.
I knew just what I wanted to do.
I could hardly wait to pour for me
A great big glass of sweet iced tea.
I looked in the fridge and came to a stop.
Someone had drunk up every last drop!

I have a shelf full of books
on organization,
But I've finally come
to the realization,
That the reason I never seem
to get around to it
Is because I'd rather
read about it than do it!

I get my life
all neatly arranged,
Then something new happens
and everything's changed.
I may be rigid
and inflexible, but
I'd much rather stay
in my comfortable rut!

Did you ever start to sit
in a low, low chair
And on the way down
wonder if it was there,
Then at last you connected
with an awkward plop
Extremely grateful
to finally stop?

As I get older I remember
What my daddy used to say,
"I know I'll ache when I get up—
I just don't know *where* I'll hurt today!"

My glasses weren't really lost.
They were just temporarily misplaced.
But the fact that they were missing
Was a fact that had to be faced.
I decided someone had moved them
And said so with a frown,
Until my glasses reappeared
In the spot where I'd put them down!

There are so many things I need to do
I don't know which to choose.
While I'm thinking it all through
I think I'll take a snooze!

Rubbing Elbows

If you ask someone to pay
They will answer without fail,
"Your money's on its way.
The check is in the mail!"

Other people bring us pleasure,
You've often heard I know—
Some bring pleasure when they come
And others when they go!

I visited my friend with things to say,
But she never let me have my way.
I just sat there silent and gawking
While she did every bit of the talking!

There are those who are chatting
and nodding with a smile
Right in the middle
of the supermarket aisle,
Blocking everyone's way—
I want you to know it.
If I had a horn on my basket,
I'd blow it!

Of all the questions wives dread to hear
One is the all-time winner.
As soon as a husband comes home from work
He wants to know, "What's for dinner?"

I cook and cook all afternoon.
Then, this is just my luck—
My kids look at their dinner
And all they say is "Yuck!"

I've observed that it seems to happen,
Much more often than not,
That a person who is always cold
Marries a person who is always hot!

The Telephone:
A Mixed Blessing

When I call and get a recording
I'm as frustrated as can be.
I want to speak to someone
Who can talk right back to me!

I dial the phone, and, in answer,
these are the words I hear,
"Press one for this, press two for that,"
And I just think, "Oh, dear!"
I don't want option one or two
or even three or four.
I need a different alternative,
but they don't offer any more.
Now what to do? Somehow I need
to make some kind of choice.
What would I give if I could hear
someone's human voice!

I went to lunch with a friend
so we'd have time to talk,
But that soon came to an end
as his cell phone began to squawk.
He talked while we were eating,
but he never talked to me.
His cell phone kept on bleating,
and he spoke to it, you see.
Now when I want to talk to him,
I know just what to do.
I won't invite him out to lunch.
I'll call his cell phone, too!

I have an answer for telemarketers
That's proven to be a winner.
I ask for their telephone number
So I can call them during their dinner!

Home Sweet Home

I'm out of supplies
and I need some more,
So I must go
to the grocery store.
Which part is hardest?
Is it loading the cart,
Unloading, putting up,
or just getting a start?
Perhaps the most difficult
part of it all
Is the price we must pay
as we make our haul!

I already know before I go
That I inevitably will
Pick from all the grocery carts
The one with the wobbly wheel.

If you do your housework
It hardly ever shows.
But if one day you let it go
Then *everybody* knows!

I'm trying to do some housecleaning,
But you would never guess
That a housecleaning fling
Could make such a mess!
What do I do with stuff?
Do I keep it or throw it away?
If I keep it, where to put it
Is the challenge of the day.

I try to empty the dirty clothes bin.
My washer's always sloshing.
But more clothes keep piling in,
And I *never* finish washing!

It's not the cooking
that I mind so much—
The mixing and the stirring
and the baking and such—
But what usually
has me all shook
Is trying to decide
just *what* to cook!

The meal is over; the dishes washed and dry.
I plop down with a great big sigh.
I'm ready for a nice rest, and then
Somebody comes in hungry again.

A woman just doesn't think like a man.
My husband doesn't understand,
When my closet isn't *literally* bare,
Why I say I have nothing to wear!

To Eat or Not to Eat

The last thing I would ever buy
Would be a talking scale.
It's bad enough that I should know;
Who wants a tattle tale?

My little dog would be much thinner
If she didn't eat so much dinner.
As I scold her, me oh my,
I realize, so would I!

I'd like to be much thinner
But I won't give up my dinner,
Or my breakfast or my lunch,
Or my snacks—I like a bunch.
So now tell me what you think:
Is it likely that I'll shrink?

You must bake or boil or broil or stew

If you want to have a healthier you.

You may sauté, steam, or roast—

A piece of fried chicken I miss the most!

I want to eat a healthy diet,
and goodness knows I've tried,
But broiled foods just can't compare
to those that are deep fried!
And how about eating oatmeal
rather than bacon, eggs, and toast?
It's not hard for me to know
which one I like the most.
I don't always eat the foods
and the way I know I should,
But I have constant conflict—
eat what's healthy or what's good!

It's not that I don't realize

The benefits of exercise.

That's not all that there is to it.

I still find it hard to *do* it!

Everybody wants to supersize.

When will they realize

If I order something small,

I don't want it large or tall?

A triple decker hamburger,
a super-sized coke—
I tell you this (and it's no joke!)—
A small coke's as large as a
giant one used to be.
The next thing super-sized
is going to be me!

All the way from appetizer
through dessert
You can see what I ate
by looking at my shirt.
With every single bite
and every single sip
I must have let a bit
of each one drip.

I crept into the kitchen
in the quiet and the dark,
Reached for the cookie jar
and my hand hit the mark.
I opened the lid
and felt all around inside.
"Oh, no! Someone's eaten
the last cookie!" I cried.

Our Little Darlings

When baby arrives, a good night's sleep
flies right out the door.
Your toddlers seek your bed at night—
and wait, there's even more.
The teen age years you're waiting up
at night 'til they come in.
Not until your kids leave home
will you sleep all night again!

We hear baby crying
deep in the night.
His pacifier has dropped
right out of sight.
"Where is it?" we cry,
searching the bed and the floor.
We can't find it!
I sure hope we have some more!

Baby's food flies through the air,
On his chair and in his hair.
It goes east, west, north and south—
Everywhere but in his mouth!

You take him to the table
and put him in his seat.
You offer him fruits and veggies,
bread and milk and meat.
You try to bribe him with the promise
of having something sweet,
But sometimes your little darling
will just refuse to eat!

When you're in a hurry
and ready to go,
Why are your children
always so slow?
They have no sense of time;
feel no need to speed,
Regardless of how much
you urge and you plead.

When you take a trip with children
Two things you'll hear, I bet.
The first one is, "How much farther?"
The second, "Are we there yet?"

"On the Road Again"

The group is in the car
and ready to go.
They're waiting on you
to start the show.
You would certainly
like to please
If only you
could find the keys!

The traffic light
ahead is green.
I carefully
survey the scene.
I drive along
with cautious dread.
When will that traffic
light turn red?
Oh, no, it's yellow—
what to do?
Slam on my brakes
or speed on through?

At the stop sign I came
to a "rolling stop".
Unfortunately I failed
to see the cop
Who was hiding
in a nearby thicket,
But, he saw me
and gave me a ticket!

You drive around a crowded mall
Until you spot a space.
Then some stranger has the gall
To grab *your* parking place!

You can have computerized directions
and a GPS,
A cell phone to guide you,
but I must confess:
I still want to have
an old fashioned map
Made out of paper
and unfolded on my lap.

Everybody Talks about the Weather

My favorite season would be spring
Except my eyes begin to sting.
And then my nose starts to run—
Hay fever spoils all the fun!

If, a few days after Easter,
I notice a smell
I won't have to guess—
I'll know all too well
That something has
been left behind—
An Easter egg or two
that no one could find.

Every time
it starts to rain
I repeat
the same refrain:
My umbrella is wherever
it last was tossed,
But when I need it,
it's always lost!

The rain leaves the trees
so fresh and green,
No dust, no dirt,
all nice and clean.
One quick shower,
and then it's passed.
I wish I could dust
my house that fast!

I'm headed to the beach
to have some fun.
I love the ocean and the sand
and lying in the sun.
But there is a problem:
I don't look so cute
At my age and stage of life
in a bathing suit!

The beach is ever so much fun
As long as there is lots of sun.
But pleasure there starts to wane
As soon as it begins to rain.

We can hardly wait for summer fun,
For kids to swim and play and run.
But as the weather begins to cool
Mothers are ever so grateful for school!

In the fall one thing is hard—
We have double duty in the yard.
The grass from summer is still growing,
So we're raking leaves *and* still mowing.

In the spring and the fall
I almost despair
Trying to decide
Just what to wear.
Will it be cool
Or will it be hot?
Will it be raining
Or will it not?
I can't plan ahead
That's too hard to do.
Does deciding what to wear
Frustrate you, too?

The weather's damp;
The trees are bare.
Winter's chill
is in the air.
Cold weather soon
it will bring.
It's a long, *long* time
from now 'til spring.

At first the snow was fluffy and nice.
Then it turned to dirty, gray ice.
We could hardly wait for it to snow.
Now we are eager to see it go!

In the winter, I dream of spring
And all the flowers it will bring—
Of daffodils and soft green grass.
Seems it will *never* come to pass.

When the weather's cold and dreary,
I wish for summer, hot and cheery.
In summer, am I pleased? I'm not!
I puff and fan and cry, "I'm hot!"

Merry
Christmas
Happy New Year

While I'm Christmas shopping
for all the others—
Children, parents,
sisters, brothers—
Somehow I always
seem to see,
And buy, some things
that are for me!

Have you ever bought a gift
with the price tag glued on?
And tried to peel and scrape it off
until the tag was gone?
But, when you've finished doing
all that you can do,
Still left behind for all to see
is the icky sticky glue?

There's one thing in the fall
that has me hopping.
This is when I start
my Christmas shopping.
It might seem to be
too early in the year,
But, before we know it,
the time will be here.
You may find this
hard to believe,
But my husband used to ask me
on CHRISTMAS EVE,
This amazing question—
"Well, my dear,
Do we have any gifts
for the children this year?"

There is hustle and bustle
Christmas time of the year.
We hardly have a minute to
enjoy Christmas cheer.
We run and we wiggle and
we shop 'til we drop.
Help! Won't somebody
please make us stop?

The store shelves were stocked
all neat and tidy
In hopes that shoppers
would come to Black Friday.
And come they did,
with elbows flying,
Rushing and shoving
and swarming and buying.
Guards were stationed at stores
to control the crowd
In case the shoppers
became too rowdy or loud
With pushing or fighting
or giving a shove
As they prepared for the season
of brotherly love.

Have you ever had this happen?
It has happened to me.
I put up and decorated
the Christmas tree.
It finally looked beautiful,
with ornaments galore,
But when I took another look,
It was lying on the floor!

Christmas is swiftly coming our way.

Soon it will be Christmas day.

Then we'll be left with a present-less tree

And all of the after Christmas debris.

My New Year's resolutions
sound familiar,
And why that is
should be very clear.
No wonder I recognize
them so easily—
They're the very same ones
I made last year!

Zingers!

I tell you
the absolute truth—
Few things hurt worse than
an unhappy tooth!

I change baby's diaper, and then
I turn around, and he's wet again!

Have you ever taught a teenager to drive?
You're always grateful to arrive alive!

Once you've opened it on your lap
It's awfully hard to refold a map!

Have you ever watched a child
lick the ice cream in a cone?
It drips and smears out to his ears
before the ice cream's gone.

Why are pounds so easy to gain
but oh so hard to lose?
I think because it's fun to eat
but oh so hard to refuse.

Making new resolutions
is no trouble any more.
I just recycle
the ones I've made before!

Quandary: When my husband
falls asleep in his chair,
Do I wake him up to go to bed
or do I leave him there?

Have you ever been roused
from a deep, peaceful slumber
By the telephone's ring—
and it was a wrong number?

When I go to bed, what should I say?
I don't know if I "lie" or "lay".

I'm afraid my mind has begun to go.
I can't remember what I know!